Baltimore County
MARYLAND
Marriage References
1659–1746

Robert Barnes

Baltimore County Genealogical Society
Special Publication #1

HERITAGE BOOKS
2011

HERITAGE BOOKS
AN IMPRINT OF HERITAGE BOOKS, INC.

Books, CDs, and more—Worldwide

For our listing of thousands of titles see our website at
www.HeritageBooks.com

Published 2011 by
HERITAGE BOOKS, INC.
Publishing Division
100 Railroad Ave. #104
Westminster, Maryland 21157

Copyright © 1988 Robert Barnes

Other books by the author:

1783 Tax List of Baltimore County
Robert W. Barnes and Bettie S. Carothers

Baltimore County, Maryland Deed Abstracts, 1659–1750

Baltimore and Fell's Point Directory of 1796

Gleanings from Maryland Newspapers, 1776–85

Gleanings from Maryland Newspapers, 1786–90

Gleanings from Maryland Newspapers, 1791–95

Index to Baltimore County Wills, 1659–1850
Robert Barnes and Bettie S. Carothers

Index to Marriages and Deaths in the Baltimore County Advocate, *1850–1864*

All rights reserved. No part of this book may be reproduced or transmitted in any form or by any means, electronic or mechanical, including photocopying, recording or by any information storage and retrieval system without written permission from the author, except for the inclusion of brief quotations in a review.

International Standard Book Numbers
Paperbound: 978-1-58549-123-0
Clothbound: 978-0-7884-8661-6

Dedicated to

Edna Agatha Kanley
for her many hours
of service in helping others

and

Richard B. Miller, Ph.D.
for his generous gifts to the
Baltimore County Genealogical Society

Thank You

USING THIS BOOK

The marriage references are arranged alphabetically by groom. Each reference is numbered. All surnames mentioned or intimated are indexed by this marriage reference number **not** by page number. Names marked with an "*" in the index indicates an heir, coheir, adminitrix, or administrator is named in that reference.

At the end of each reference the source citations are given in parentheses. The first number is the serial number assigned to the source provided. The number following the colon is the page or folio number. A complete list of Source References is provided within this book.

ACKNOWLEDGEMENTS

This book would not have been possible without the seminal work of Richard B. Miller, Ph.D. in abstracting the earliest volumes of Baltimore County land records. His generosity in donating his notes for the use of members of the Baltimore County Genealogical Society have and will continue to be of great benefit to all.

SOURCE REFERENCES

Baltimore County Land Records (abstracted by Richard B. Miller, Ph.D.)

1 - Liber RM # HS	8 - Liber TR # A	15 - Liber HWS # M
2 - Liber IR # PP	9 - Liber TR # DS	16 - Liber HWS #1-A
3 - Liber IS # IK	10 - Liber IS # G	17 - Liber TB # A
4 - Liber G # J	11 - Liber IS # H	18 - Liber TB # C
5 - Liber TR # RA	12 - Liber IS # J	19 - Liber TB # D
7 - Liber HW # 2	13 - Liber IS # K	20 - Liber TB # E
	14 - Liber IS # L	

Baltimore County Administration Accounts (abstracted by Robert W. Barnes)

21 or 41 - Liber 1	23 or 43 - Liber 3	25 or 45 Liber - 5
22 or 42 - Liber 2	24 or 44 - Liber 4	46 Liber - 6

26 - <u>Maryland Rent Rolls: Baltimore and Anne Arundel Counties</u> (Baltimore Genealogical Publishing Company, 1976)

Baltimore County Court Proceedings (abstracted by Robert W. Barnes)

27 - Liber D	1682-1686	30 - Liber IS B, 1708-1715
28 - Liber F #1	1691-1693	31 - Liber IS # !A, 1715-1718
29 - Liber G #1	1693-1696	32 - Liber IS # C, 1718-1721

Numbers 33-40 not used.

Baltimore County Inventories (abstracted by Robert W. Barnes)

47 - Liber 1	49 - Liber 3	51 - Liber 5
48 - Liber 2	50 - Liber 4	

BALTIMORE COUNTY MARRIAGE REFERENCES, 1659-1746

BY
ROBERT W. BARNES

Each marriage reference is numbered. The references are indexed by number and not by page number. Documentation is given in parentheses after the reference. Check the list of references to see where the marriage reference was found.

1. Adams, Richard m. by Dec. 1691, Mary, admnx. of John Stansby (28:146).
2. Addision (---), of Prince Georges Co., m. by 30 Sept. 1727, Eleanor, sister of Richard Smith of Calvert Co. (12:6)
3. Andrews, William, m. by 23 Aug. 1742, (---), daughter of William Bond (43:271).
4. Arding, or Harding, (---) m. by 1714, Mary, heir of Joseph Strawbridge (41.7)
5. Arnold, Benjamin, m: by 1696, (---), widow of James Phillips (Inv. and Accts. 15:25; 42:63)
6. Ashman, (---), m. by 28 Oct 1743, Jemina, daughter of Josephus Murray (18:340)
7. Ashman, George, m. by 1702/3 (when he was dead), Elizabeth, widow of William Cromwell, and mother of Thomas Cromwell (41:349; 42:244)
8. Ashman, John, m. by 4 May 1722, (---), daughter of John Wilmot (41:253)
9. Askew, Richard, m. by 4 March 1690, Mary, widow and extx. of Edward Reeves (6:68; 28:128: 129:84)
10. Bacon, Martin, m. by 15 Oct. 1742, Mary, mother of William Watson (18:55)
11. Bagby, John, of Calvert Co., m. by 30 Aug. 1719, Mary, daughter of John Ford (9:147)
12. Bailey, George, m. by 26 Oct. 1741, Rachel, extx. of John Moale (17:30)
13. Bailey, John, m. by 1 Sept. 1739, Helen Nusome (16:271)
14. Ball, Richard, m. by 1 March 1661, Mary, widow of Thomas Humphreys (1:19; <u>Arch.Md.</u>, 67:134)
15. Barnes, (---), m. by 18 Feb. 1722/3, Constant, daughter of Robert West (10:94)
16. Barnes, James, m. by 18 April 1723, Keturah, daughter of Adam Shipley (8:242)

BALTIMORE COUNTY MARRIAGE REFERENCES 1659 - 1746

17. Barnes, James, m. by 23 Dec 1742, (---), daughter of William Loney (43:274)
18. Barnes, (---), m. by 16 Jan 1717 Elizabeth, daughter of Mary Stevenson (20:517)
19. Barton, John, m. by 5 Dec.1744, Ann, daughter of William Hitchcock (18:664)
20. Beal, John, m. by 9 Oct. 1724, Elizabeth, sister of Andrew Norwood (10:387)
21. Beason, Nicholas, m. by 12 Dec. 1722, Diana, admnx. of William Hutchings and of Mathew Hale or Hall (1:73)
22. Beaven, John, m. by 3 Nov. 1692, Sarah, widow of Benjamin Bennett (1:361)
23. Beaver, William, Jr., m. by 10 Oct. 1741, Blanch, daughter of William Duley (44:110)
24. Beck, Matthew, m. by 13 Nov. 1741, Ann, Admnx. of Nicholas Horner (44:112)
25. Belcher, John, m. by 1 July 1708, Mary, widow of Richard Perkins (40:88, 93)
26. Bell, John, m. by 29 July 1746, Susanna, daughter of John Tye (20:119)
27. Benger, (---), m. by 31 March 1744, Deborah, mother of Jane Johnson (who m: Daniel Scott), and of Elizabeth Shaw (18:471)
28. Benger, Robert, m. Katherine, admnx. of John Shadwell (42.41)
29. Bentley, Stephen, m. by Nov. 1693, Ann, relict of Phillip Piffions (?), and formerly wife of William Pearle (28:300, 307)
30. Billingsley, Walter, m. by 4 Sept. 1742, Sarah, widow of Robert Love (18:5)
31. Bird, John, m. by Nov. 1684, (---), widow of James Armstrong (27:212)
32. Bisco, (---), m. by 2 May 1732, Ann, daughter of Thomas Jackson; she m. 2nd Owen Smithson (14:256)
33. Bishop, Robert, m. by 22 May 1746, Elizabeth widow of Nicholas Day, and daughter of Christopher and Mary Cox (20:63)
34. Bolton, (---), m. by 10 Feb. 1684, Elizabeth, late wife of Richard Bennett of Anne Arundel Co. (1:110)
35. Bolton, Charles, m. by 11 Oct. 1739, Ann, admnx of John Higginson (44:26)
36. Bolton, John, m. by Nov 1685, Dorothy Crandon (27:358)
37. Bond, Benjamin, m. by 20 July 1740, Clemency, daughter of Martin Taylor, whose widow Sarah m. Robert Robertson (44:53)

BALTIMORE COUNTY MARRIAGE REFERENCES 1659 - 1746

38. Bond, John, m. by 26 Feb. 1712/3, Mary, admnx. of Samuel Standiver or Standiford (41:370; 42:172)39.
39. Bond, Peter, m. by 8 March 1730, (---), daughter of Isaac Butterworth (44:12)
40. Booker, John, m. by Sept 1694, Edith, extx. of Christopher Gist (29:289)
41. Boone, John, m. by 1705, (---), widow of John Durham, only daughter of Francis Tripolls (1:553; 6:60)
42. Boothy, Edward, m. by 7 July 1708, Elizabeth, widow and admnx. of Capt. Henry Johnson (42:118)
43. Boreing, James, m. by 4 March 1719, Jane, daughter and coheir of Daniel Welsh (9:196)
44. Boreing, James, m. by 15 June 1739, Martha, daughter of William Wheeler (44:35)
45. Bosley, Charles, m. by 3 Aug. 1736, Elizabeth, daughter of William Cox (15:418)
46. Bosworth, (---), m. by 3 Dec. 1745, Mary, daughter of William Robinson (19:428)
47. Bowen, Benjamin, m. by Nov. 1710, Mary, widow and admnx. of Nathaniel Ruxton (30:187)
48. Bowen, John, m. by 10 May 1746, Milcah (Milia or Mildor?), daughter of Robert Clarkson (1:549, 566).
49. Bowen, John, m. by 22 Jan. 1742, Rosanna, widow of James Robertson (18:96)
50. Boyd, Robert, m. by 6 Dec. 1742, Ruth Bays heir of Christopher Shaw (18:223)
51. Brangwell, Peter, m. by 30 April (1683?), Elizabeth Kemb (27:94)
52. Brashiers, Thomas, m. by 2 Nov. 1726, Sarah, daughter of John Constant, Sr. (11:381)
53. Broad, (---), m. by 11 Aug. 1712, Barbara, widow of (---) Cole (8:221)
54. Broad, John, m. by Nov 1692, Barbara, relict of Dennis Garrett (28:276)
55. Broad, John, m. by 13 Oct 1739, Jemima, granddaughter of Joseph Peake (16:336)
56. Broad, Thomas, m. by 23 Sept. 1723, Anna, prob. daughter and coheir of Matthew Hawkins (10:208)
57. Brown, Joshua, m. by 14 Jan. 1722, Margaret, sister of William Chew of Baltimore Co. (41:109)

BALTIMORE COUNTY MARRIAGE REFERENCES 1659 - 1746

58. Brown, Nicholas, m. by 16 Sept. 1687, Ann, orig. admins. of Dennis English (Inv. and Accts., IX, 427)
59. Buchanan, Archibald, m. by 30 Sept. 1706, Mary, widow of Thomas Preble (42:233)
60. Buchanan, Archibald, m. by 19 June 1731, daughter of John Roberts (43:99)
61. Buck, Edward, m. by 3 Aug. 1713, Jane, admnx. of John Anderson (41:223)
62. Duckner, William, m. by 10 Jan. 1726/7, Patience, daughter of Col. Richard Colegate (41:322)
63. Burchfield, Thomas, m. c.4 Aug. 1721, Joan, extx. of Edward Cantwell (41:258)
64. Burk, James, m. by 26 Oct. 1741, Ann, extx. of Christopher Randall (17:30)
65. Burney, William, m. by 4 Nov. 1719, Martha, relict and sole extx. of William Howard (9:60)
66. Burroughs, Richard, m. by March 1716/7 Eliz., relict of John Brown (31:93)
67. Byfoot, William, m. by 5 March 1744, Sarah, daughter of John Hall (19:51)
68. Caggill, John, m. by 13 Oct. 1739, Mary, granddaughter of Joseph Peake (16:336)
69. Cannon, (---), m. by 15 Dec. 1721, Barbara, daughter of John Fitzredmond (50:206)
70. Cannon, Robert, m. by 23 Oct. 1736, (---), daughter of Daniel Johnson (43:224)
71. Cannon, William m. by 23 Oct. 1736, (---), daughter of Daniel Johnson (43:244)
72. Carr, John, m. by 30 March 1744, Lewsey, coheir of John Clark who was a son of Matthew Clark (18:565)
73. Carroll, Peter, m. by 6 March 1744. Ann, formerly wife of William Hitchcock (18:671)
74. Carson, William, m. by 20 Sept. 1744, Elizabeth, sister of Andrew Johnson (18:601)
75. Carvill, John, m. by 20 July 1701, Mary, daughter of Susanna Arnold (7:57)
76. Chadbourne, William, m. by 13 Dec. 1674, (---), relict of Richard Foxon or Fexton (42:202)

BALTIMORE COUNTY MARRIAGE REFERENCES 1659 - 1746

77. Chancey, George, m. after 1700, (---), daughter of William Hollis (26:23)
78. Chancey, George, m. by 2 Feb. 1707/8, Sarah, admins. of Benjamin Smith (42:171)
79. Clarke, Matthew, m. (as 2nd wife?), by 30 March 1744, Elizabeth, sister of James Ford (18:565)
80. Cobb, James, m. by 9 Oct. 1710 or 1719, Rebecca, extx. of James Emison (42:147)
81. Cockey, (---), m. by 3 March 1719, Sarah, widow of Thomas Hanson (9:95)
82. Cole, John, m. by 23 Sept. 1723, Diana, prob. daughter and coheir of Matthew Hawkins (10:208)
83. Colegate, Benjamin, m. by 15 Sept. 1741, Charity, daughter of Benjamin Wheeler (16:557)
84. Colegate, Richard, m. by 5 Aug. 1707, Rebecca, daughter of Eleanor Herbert (1:569)
85. Coleman Duncan, m. by 16 April 1731, Sarah, widow of Thomas Towson (43:85)
86. Collier, John, m. by 9 March 1673, Ann, widow of James Stringer of Anne Arundel Co. (Testamentary Proceedings, 6:42)
87. Collier, John, m. by March 1684/5, Sarah, admnx. of George Hooper; she m. 3rd, by 1 April 1693, John Hall (7:38; 27:252)
88. Collison, William, m. by 13 April 1715, Susannah, admnx. of William Addams (41:212)
89. Cook, (---), m. by 22 Feb 1727, Sarah, daughter of Robert West (11:395)
90. Copas, John, m. by Nov. 1685, Ann, widow of Matthew Wood (27:356)
91. Copus, John, m. b 30 March 1699, Sarah Teale, mother of Ales Teale (5:338)
92. Cord, Abraham, m. by 15 March 1735, Mary, sister of Joseph Pritchard, dec. (15:401)
93. Corne, Thomas, m. by Aug. 1714, Elizabeth, extx. of John Mortimore (30:566)
94. Cornelius, John, m. by March 1719, Sarah, admnx. of Stephen White (32:342)
95. Cosden, Alphonso, m. by 12 March 1724, Ann, daughter of Christopher Beanes of Calvert Co. (11:101)
96. Cox, Edward, m. by 7 June 1723, Jane, daughter of John Broad (10:194)
97. Cresap, Thomas, m. by 23 Oct 1736, (---). daughter of Daniel Johnson (43:224)

BALTIMORE COUNTY MARRIAGE REFERENCES 1659 - 1746

98. Cromwell, Thomas, m. by 11 Oct. 1709, Jemima, extx. of James Murray (42:207, 208)
99. Croshaw, William, d. by Aug. 1685, having m. Elizabeth Russell, whom m. by that date William Harris (27:385)
100. Cross, Henry, m. by 6 Aug. 1747, Mary, widow of John Royston, dec. (20:497)
101. Curtis, Benjamin, m. by 28 July 1744, Abigail or Abarilla, admins. of Nicholas Gostwick (43:360)
102. Cutchin, Robert, m. by 11 Nov. 1702, Dorothy; admins. of Moses Grooms (41:83)
103. Cutchin, Thomas, m. by Aug. 1715, Jane Hicks (30:633)
104. Dallahide, (---), m. by 10 Dec. 1740, Mary, mother of John Bradshaw of Prince Georges Co. (16:470)
105. Dallas, Walter, m. by 24 Oct. 1732, Chloe, daughter of James Crock (43:115)
106. Davies, Vaughn, of New York, N.Y., m. by 2 Dec. 1723, Catherine, only daughter and heir of Gideon Skates, dec. (10:283)
107. Dawkins, William, of Calvert Co., m. by 19 Nov. 1724, Ann, daughter of Richard Smith of Calvert Co. (11:22)
108. Dawney, John, m. by 6 July 1723, Lydia, daughter of Mark Swift, Sr. (10:265)
109. Day, Nicholas, m. by 22 May 1746, Elizabeth, daughter of Christopher and Mary Cox; Day was dec. by that date and his widow had m. 2nd Robert Bishop (20:63)
110. Debruler, John, m. by 5 March 1728, Mary, daughter of Thomas Greenfield (12:266)
111. Demasters, Anthony, m. by Nov. 1692, Rebecca, widow of Randall Death (28:325)
112. Denton, James, m. by Aug. 1684, Rebecca, widow of Thomas O'Daniel (27:164)
113. Devega, John, m. by Sept. 1693, Elizabeth, admnx. of William Dison (29:103)
114. Devegha, John, m. by 7 Nov. 1694, Elizabeth, daughter of Edmund Ayres (1:439)
115. Doddridge, William, m. by 23 Dec. 1717, Lettice, daughter of Abraham Taylor (5:435)
116. Donovan, Thomas, m. by 5 March 1744, Frances, daughter of John Hall (19:51)

BALTIMORE COUNTY MARRIAGE REFERENCES 1659 - 1746

117. Dorman, Selah, m. by 8 March 1698, Jane, heir of Roger Sidwell (5:325)
118. Dorrumple, John, of Calvert Co., m. by 20 July 1738, Elinor, daughter of William Harris (16:123)
119. Dorsey, John, of Cecil Co., m. by 11 Dec. 1727, Sylvia, widow of John Heathcote (12:82)
120. Dottridge, (---), m. by 1 Aug. 1721, (---) daughter of Abraham Taylor (41:285)
121. Dowell, Phillip, m. by 4 April 1747, Mary, daughter of Richard Tydings (20:522)
122. Downs, John, m. by March 1711/2, Mary, admnx. of Christopher Durbin (30:308)
123. Dunkin, John, m. by 26 March 1694, Ann, daughter of John Mould (1:422)
124. Durbin, John, m. by 9 July 1725, Avarilla, daughter of Daniel Scott (43:18)
125. Durbin, Samuel, m. by 19 Sept. 1726, Ann, daughter of Willliam Logsdon (11:338)
126. Durham, James, m. by 5 June 1693/4, Mary, daughter of John Lee (1:390)
127. Durham, James, m. by 2 Oct. 1707, Margaret, extx. and widow of William Galloway, and sister of Abraham Enloes (42:182; 47:6; 30:125)
128. Durham, John, m. by Nov 1683, Jane, admnx. of William Choice (26:13, 14)
129. Elliott, Phillip Lackey, m. Sarah, admnx. of William Wright (45:286)
130. Emory, Robert, m. by 14 March 1722/6, Ann, widow of William Hawkins (41:146)
131. Ensor, John, m. by March 1709, Elizabeth, admnx. of Abraham Enloes (30:133)
132. Erickson, Erick, m. by 8 April 1730, Mary, widow and devisee of Robert Smith (13:210)
133. Evans, Edward, m. by 2 June 1725, Rachel Johnson, admnx. of John Hastings (43:45; 50:215)
134. Evans, Evan, m. by 23 Oct. 1736, (---), daughter of Daniel Johnson (43:224)
135. Everest Thomas, of the Cliffs, Calvert Co., m. by 11 Feb. 1683, Hannah, daughter and heiress of Richard Ball (1:74)

BALTIMORE COUNTY MARRIAGE REFERENCES 1659 - 1746

136. Ewings, John, m. by 29 Jan. 1708, Elizabeth, sister of Moses Groome (1:633)
137. Everett, John, m. by 9 March 1732, Rebecca, daughter of John Poteet (14:337)
138. Farfarr, William, m. by Nov. 14, 1714, Eleanor, admnx. of John Harryman (30:598)
139. Farlow, Thomas, m. by 18 Nov. 1738, Elizabeth, widow of James Little (44:5)
140. Felkes, Edward, m. by 11 Feb. 1704, Ann, former wife of Stephen Johnson and kinswoman of Moses Groome (2:171; 7:119; 42:27)
141. Fitzsimmons, Nicholas, m. by Sept. 1693, Martha, extx. of Joseph Heathcote (29:116, 152)
142. Ford, Abraham, m. by 17 Feb. 1736, Mary, sister of Joseph Pritchard (3:358)
143. Fottrell, Edward, m. by 22 July 1741, Achsah, admnx. of Amos Woodward (44:86)
144. Fouracres, Laurence, m. by 10 March 1730, Rachel, daughter of William Hill of Cecil Co. (14:211)
145. Foy, (---), m. by 27 Oct. 1736 Frances, extx. of Daniel Johnwon (43:224)
146. Foy, Miles, antenuptual contract dated 4 Oct. 1728, Frances, widow of Hugh Grant (12:317)
147. Frazer, John, d. by 6 Jan. 1717, having m. Mary, widow of Dennis Duskins (5:523)
148. Frazer, John, m. by 17 March 1742, Rebecca, admnx. of James Boreing (43:256; 44:122)
149. Friend (or Howard), James, m. by March 1683/4, Jane, relict of Ambrose Gillett (27:141)
150. Frisby, William, m. by 4 Aug. 1719, daughter of G. Wells (41:54)
151. Frizzell, James, m. by Nov. 1692, Mary, mother of William York (28:316)
152. Fucatt, Peter, m. by 4 July 1694, Frances, daughter of John Mould (1:419)
153. Gadd, (---), m. by 25 March 1742, Christiana, mother of Abraham Ditto (18:195)
154. Garrett, Bennett, m. by 2 April 1736, Arabella, daughter of John Walston; on 10 Sept. 1741 she was called admnx. of William Loney (15:424; 43:274; 44:297)

BALTIMORE COUNTY MARRIAGE REFERENCES 1659 - 1746

155. Garrett, Henry, m. by 9 Aug. 1745, Mary, daughter of Isaac Butterworth (19:300)
156. Garrettson, John, m. by 21 Aug. 1745, Sarah Hanson, granddaughter of Sarah Cockey who was later Sarah Tayman (19:311)
157. Garrison, (---), m. by 13 June 1720, Elizabeth, sister of Richard Freeborne (1:661)
158. Gay, John, m. by 3 Sept. 1701, Frances, heir of Nathaniel Ruxton (7:90)
159. Gears, Daniel, of Cecil Co., m. by 5 Aug. 1723, Elizabeth, daughter of Daniel Benson of Anne Arundel Co. (10:172)
160. Geoghegan, Ambrose, m. by 8 Sept. 1724, Katherine, extx. of Pierce Welch (42:369)
161. Gibson, Miles, m. c.19 May 1676, Anne, daughter of Thomas Thurston (4:330)
162. Gilbert, (---), m. by March 1721/3, Rebecca, mother of Sarah Howe (Baltimore Co. Court Proc., Liber IS#TW#I, p.16)
163. Gilbert, Michael, m. by 15 Dec. 1739, Mary, daughter of Martin Taylor (16:324)
164. Giles, Jacob, m. by 7 Dec. 1739, Johannah, daughter of Col. James Phillips (16:310)
166. Giles, John, of ANNE ARUNDEL Co., m. by 17 March 1708, Sarah, daughter of John Welsch (8:5)
165. Gillibourn, Thomas, m. by March 1691/2, Mary, relict of Timothy Pinder (28:164)
167. Gist, Richard, m. by 6 July 1711, Zipporah, sister of Josephus Murray (5:444; 8:140)
168. Gist, Nathaniel, m. by 8 Jan. 1739, Mary, heir of Joshua Howard (44:440)
169. Gist, William, m. by 8 Jan. 1739, Violetta, heir of Joshua Howard (44:40)
170. Gorsuch, Charles, of Talbot Co., m. by 8 Dec. 1679, Sarah, heiress of the lands of Thomas Cole (2:46)
171. Gray, Zachariah, m. by 24 Dec. 1730, Rebecca, daughter of Jonas Bowen (18:464)
172. Green, (---), m. by 5 May 1700, Elizabeth, daughter of Anthony Demondidier (7:51)
173. Green, (---), m. by 4 March 1745/6, Susannah, daughter of Nicholas Haile (20:10)

BALTIMORE COUNTY MARRIAGE REFERENCES 1659 - 1756

174. Green, Matthew, m. by 1 Aug. 1719, Mary, daughter of Jane Boone (9:42)
175. Greeniff, John, m. by 4 Nov, 1703, Ruth, extx. of Edward Dorsey of Capt. John (42:228)
176. Greer, James, m. by 24 June 1742, Elizabeth, widow of William Wright; she m. 3rd by 27 July 1743 Heathcote Pickett (43:267, 312)
177. Griffith, Samuel, m. by 21 April 1741, Mary, sister of Luke Raven (16:490)
178. Grover, George, m. by 1 May 1724, Jane Russell, who had an inheritance in Va. (10:312)
179. Grundy, Robert, m. Mary or Margaret, extx. of John Pemberton (41:288)
180. Gunnell, George, m. by July 1699, Jane, admnx. of Thomas Overton (42:72)
181. Hacks, Jeremiah, m. Mary, adminx. of John Clark (42:107)
182. Hall, (---), m. by 9 Aug. 1688, Sarah, extx. of Abraham Holman (Md.Inv. and Accts., 10:169)
183. Hall, John, m. by March 1684/5, Sarah, admnx. of George Hooper, and widow of John Collier; in April 1693 she was called mother of Isabella Hooper and Ann Collier (7:38)
184. Hall, John, m. by Dec. 1696, Martha, daughter of Edward Bedell; extx of George Goldsmith (3:80; 29:205)
185. Hall, John, m. by 27 Oct. 1735, Hannah, extx. of Abraham Johns (42:214)
186. Hall, John, m. by 7 May 1741, Hannah, widow of Asael Maxwell (44:75)
187. Hall, William, m. by 23 June 1727, Mary, widow of Thomas Gwins (43:92)
188. Hammond, (---), m. by 5 Oct. 1746, Sarah, daughter of Thomas Sheredine (20:185)
189. Hammond, Benjamin, m. by 17 June 1743, Margaret, daughter of William Talbott (18:351)
190. Hammond, Lawrence, m. by 28 Feb. 1742, Avarilla, daughter of John Simkins (18:169)
191. Hammond, Thomas, m. by 21 Feb. 1693, Rebecca, widow of Thomas Lightfoot (1:417)
192. Hand, or Stand, John, m. by 14 Feb. 1732, Rosanna, daughter of Jacob Grove (43:108)

BALTIMORE COUNTY MARRIAGE REFERENCES 1659 - 1746

193. Hanson, Jacob, m. by 13 Jan. 1743, Mary or Margaret, daughter of Samuel Hughes (18:380)
194. Hanson, Jonathan, m. by 4 Nov. 1726, Mary, daughter of Mordecai and Mary Price (42:303)
195. Hardesty, Joshua, m. by 2 Jan. 1747, Keziah, extx. of John Taylor (44:176)
196. Harmer, Godfrey, m. by 20 June 1662, Mary, daughter of Oliver Sprye (1:10)
197. Harman, William, m. by 1 Sept. 1744, Sarah, mother of Edward Powell (18:587)
198. Harriet, Oliver, m. by 13 June 1711, Ann, admnx. of Lawrence Richardson (42:2)
199. Harris, James, m. by 2 Nov. 1718, Bathsheba, daughter of James Barlow (42:311)
200. Harris, Lloyd, m. by 20 Nov. 1724, Ellinor, extx. of Nicholas Rogers (42:349). In Nov. 1724 she was called extx of Jabez Pierpoint (43:1, 9)
201. Harris, William, m. by March 1684/5, relict and admnx. of William Hollis (27:240)
202. Harris, William, m. by Aug. 1685, Elizabeth (formerly Russell), widow of William Crashow (27:385)
203. Harrison, John, m. by 27 March 1719, Margaret, widow of Daniel McIntosh (41:49)
204. Harryman, Thomas, m. by 10 April 1729, Eliz. extx. of John Norton
205. Hatch, John, m. by 3 July 1710 Sarah, admns, of Edward Jones (42:158)
206. Hawkins, Matthew, m. by 11 Oct. 1745, Elizabeth, sister of Thomas Francis Roberts (19:374)
207. Hawkins, William, m. by 18 Oct. 1722, Judith, extx. of George Hope (43:81)
208. Hayes, (---), m. by 4 June 1728, Grace, daughter of William Crabtree (13:20)
209. Hayes, Edmund, m. by Nov. 1710, Mary Mencham, formerly bound to Nathaniel Ruxton (30:87)
210. Hays, John, m. by 31 Oct. 1727, Mary, daughter of William Crabtree (13:20)
211. Head, Bigger, of Calvert Co., m. by 22 Jan. 1745, Martha, coheir of Edward Butler, dec. (20:1)
212. Heighe, Samuel, m. by 24 July 1727, Sarah, relict of John Israel (12:29)

11

BALTIMORE COUNTY MARRIAGE REFERENCES 1659 - 1746

213. Hemstead, Nicholas, m. by 2 Sept. 1679, Elizabeth (---), grandmother of Enoch Spinke (7:159)
214. Hendon, (---), m. by 3 Dec. 1745, Hannah, daughter of William Robinson (19:428)
215. Herrington, Cornelius, m. by 25 April 1701, Rathvael (Rachel?), daughter of Thomas Jones (7:105)
216. Hewett, (---), m. by Nov. 1721, Mary, daughter of Thomas Williamson (32:626)
217. Hewling, Jonas, dec., m. by 12 July 1736, Ann, mother of Patrick Lynch (15:417)
218. Hicks, Nehemiah, m. by 6 March 1727, Philisana, daughter of William Hitchcock, dec. (12:57)
219. Hill, William, m. by 3 March 1732, Martha, daughter and coheir of Matthew Green (14:326)
220. Hillen, John, m. by Nov. 1708, Margaret or Mary, admnx. of Thomas James (30:18; 42:170)
221. Hillen, Solomon, m. by 21 April 1741, Elizabeth, sister of Luke Raven (16:490)
222. Hitchcock, George, m. by Aug. 1714, Mary, admnx. of Tego O'Tracey (30:547)
223. Holland, Francis, m. by 28 Feb. 1716, Susanna, daughter of George Utie (8:437)
224. Holland, Otho, of Anne Arundel Co., m. by 3 Aug. 1719, Mary, late wife of Charles Howard of Anne Arundel Co. (9:157)
225. Hollis, William, m. by Nov. 1692, Mary, daughter of Abraham and Sarah Clarke (1:401; 28:310)
226. Hopham, William, m. by 7 March 1722, Jane; admins. of George Newport (51:27)
227. Hopkins, William, m. by 2 Nov. 1742, Rachel, extx. of Charles Daniel (43:296)
228. Horne, Thomas, m. by 8 Nov. 1743, daughter of Abigail Barton (18:363)
229. Horne, William, m. by 5 Nov. 1684, Mary, daughter of Thomas O'Daniel (1:101)
230. Houckings, William, m. by 9 Dec. 1724, Judith, extx. of George Hope (11:89)
231. Howard, Gideon, m. by 23 Oct. 1723, Hannah, admins. of William Orrick (41:116)

BALTIMORE COUNTY MARRIAGE REFERENCES 1659 - 1746

232. Howard, Lemuel, m. by 9 Jan. 1744, Anne, widow of Edward Howard (18:668)
233. Howard, Thomas, m. by 15 April 1724, Catherine, widow of Anthony Johnson, and mother of William Johnson (10:273)
234. Howard (or Friend), James, m. by March 1683/4, Jane, relict of Ambrose Gillett (27:141)
235. Howell, Samuel, m. by 27 June 1721, Priscilla, extx. of Richard Freeborne (41:244, 260)
236. Hubbard, John, m. by 1680, Margaret, relict and admnx. of John Leakins (42:45)
237. Huggins, James, of Cecil Co., m. by 5 Aug. 1723, Jane, daughter of Daniel Benson of Anne Arundel Co. (10:172)
238. Hughes, Caleb, m. by 17 Feb. 1740, Hester, admnx. of Peter Bond (44:30, 61)
239. Hughes, David, m. by 19 June 1731, Mary, extx. of John Roberts (43:99)
240. Hughes, John, m. by 10 Dec. 1747, Elizabeth, daughter of Benjamin Norris (20:637)
241. Hughes, Jonathan, m. by 4 Nov. 1742, Jane, daughter of Martin Taylor, Jr. (18:164)
242. Hughes, Samuel, m. by 9 July 1725, Jane, daughter of Daniel Scott (43:18)
243. Hughes, William, m. by 26 April 1738, Hannah, admnx. of Joseph Bankson (44:15)
244. Hughs, David, m. by 13 Nov. 1738, Mary, relict of John Roberts and mother of Lucina Roberts (16:140)
245. Humphrey, Richard, m. by 12 July 1715, Elizabeth; admins. of Henry Jones (41:336)
246. Humphries, Richard, m. by March 1719, Elizabeth, admnx. of Henry Jones (30:342)
247. Hunter, William, m. by 20 April 1722, Mary, execs. of John Webster (41:66)
248. Husbands, William, m. by 3 Oct 1716, Mary Brooke, admnx. of Thomas Currier (41:207)
249. Hutchins, Thomas, m. by March 1709, Susanna, extx. of Thomas Richardson (30:120)
250. Hutchinson, William, of Prince Georges Co., m. by 6 July 1722, Sarah, daughter of Robert Doyne of Charles Co. (10:88)

BALTIMORE COUNTY MARRIAGE REFERENCES 1659 1- 1746

251. Isham, James, m. by June 1719, Mary, admnx. of William Robinson (11:172); 32:162)
252. Israel, John, m. by 15 Oct. 1706, Margaret, widow and extx. of Col. Edward Dorsey (42:241)
253. Isum, James, m. by c.1703, (---), widow and admnx. of Abraham Delap (42:189)
254. Jacks, Thomas, m. by 15 Aug. 1726, Elizabeth, widow of (---) Powell (11:276)
255. James, Thomas, m. by Dec. 1691, Mary, extx. of Edward Dower or Dowse (28:111)
256. James, Thomas, of Concord, Chester Co., PA., m. by 26 June 1696, Mary, widow of Giles Stevens and mother of Giles Stevens (1:524, 529, 530; 42:35)
257. Johns, Richard, of the Cliffs, Calvert Co., m. by 10 June 1685, Elizabeth, sister of Paul Kinsey (1:154, 253)
258. Johnson, Henry, d. by 11 June 1694; m. Elizabeth, widow of Nathaniel Utie; she m. 3rd Edward Boothby (Inv. and Accts., 12:147)
259. Johnson, Samuel, m. by June 1742, Mary, widow of Garvis Gilbert (Baltimore Co. Court Proc., TR#TR, p.442)
260. Johnson, Stephen, m. by 19 Feb. 1701/2, Ann, kinswoman of Moses Groome (2:171; 7:119; 42:27)
261. Johnson, Thomas, m. by 3 Nov. 1730, Else, daughter of William Bond (14:56)
262. Johnson, Thomas, m. by 23 Aug. 1742, (---), daughter of William Bond (43:271)
263. Jones, Benjamin, m. by 2 April 1728, Elizabeth, daughter of William Pickett (12:64)
264. Jones, David, m. by 16 Jan. 1678, (---), relict of Thomas Todd (47:284)
265. Jones, John, m. by 25 July 1724, Margaret, daughter and sole heir of John Chadwell, Sr. (10:352)
266. Jones, John, m. by 27 July 1733, Hannah, daughter of John Wooley (14:405)
267. Jones, Thomas, m. by 1696, Mary Harrison, legatee of Edward Dowse (1:524)
268. Judd, Michael, m. by 2 Aug. 1681, Jane, former wife of William Ebden and mother of William Ebden (1:348; 28:165)

BALTIMORE COUNTY MARRIAGE REFERENCES 1659 1- 1746

269. Keith, Alexander, m. by 26 Feb. 1708/9, Christiana, daughter of William Farfarr (1:636)
270. Kemp, John, m. by 13 Oct 1739, Mary, granddaughter of Joseph Peake (16:336)
271. Keon, (---), of N.C., m. by 6 June 1711, Hannah, formerly wife of Lodowick Williams (9:135)
272. King, (---), m. by 24 June 1702, Gavilla (?), daughter of Jane Long (42:216)
273. Knight, Benjamin, m. by 22 Aug. 1729, Jane, extx. of Charles Merryman, Jr. (42:272)
274. Knowles, (---), m. by 15 Dec. 1743, Mary Fugate (18:440)
275. Knowles, Henry, m. by c1700, Catherine, widow of John Scutt (26:81)
276. Lafee, Lewis, m. by 2 April 1745, Sarah, extx. of William Love (45:35)
277. Lake, Abraham, m. by 31 March 1725, Sarah, admnx. of James Holliday (43:31)
278. Lane, Dutton, m. by 4 April 1747, Pretitia, daughter of Richard Tydings (20:522)
279. Langley, William, m. by 2 Oct. 1725, Elinor, daughter of Solomon Jones, of St. Mary's Co., dec. (11:183)
280. Lanham, Josias, m. by 24 Feb. 1720, Susannah, daughter of Anthony Drew (41:151)
281. Leakins, John, m. by 1708, Elizabeth; admins. of John Enloes (42:230)
282. Legoe, Benjamin, m. by 25 Sept. 11707, Mary, extx. of William Hill (42:169)
283. Lenox, James, m. by 22 Jan. 1735, Mary, daughter of Robuck Lynch (15:371)
284. Lenox, Richard, m. by 6 March 1705/6, Mary Richardson, sister of James Richardson (6:40; 9:212)
285. Lenox, Richard, m. by 27 Jan. 1724, Tamar Wilkinson, admnx. of Francis Keys (41:94; 42:335)
286. Lenox, William, m. by 24 Feb. 1720, Bethia, daughter of Anthony Drew (41:151)
287. Lester, George, m. by 29 Aug. 1741, Alice, admnx. of John Lea (44:118)
288. Litton, Isaac, m. by 12 May 1740 or 1746, Mary, admnx. of Thomas Jones (44:132)
289. Litton, Thomas, Jr., m. by 30 Sept. 1742, Margaret, admins. of Seaborn Tucker (43:294)

BALTIMORE COUNTY MARRIAGE REFERENCES 1659 - 1746

290. Loney, William, m. by 22 April 1700, Jane, daughter and sole heir of Thomas Overton (7:54, 220)
291. Love, or Lowe, (---), m. by 23 Aug. 1742, Sarah, daughter of William Bond (43:271)
292. Love, Robert, m. by June 1693, Sarah, daughter of Thomas Thurston (28:415, 489)
293. Love, Robert, m. by 3 Nov. 1730, Sarah, daughter of William Bond (14:58)
294. Lowe, Thomas, m. by 24 April 1704, Eliza, admnx. of John Shields (41:346)
295. Lowe, William, m. by 14 Oct. 1726, Temperance, daughter of William Pickett (18:522; 42:318)
296. Lynch, James, m. by 12 April 1747, Margaret, daughter of Mary Gittings (20:340)
297. Lynch, Patrick, m. by 24 Dec. 1730, Martha, daughter of Jonas Bowen (18:464)
298. Lynch, William, m. by 4 Aug. 1741, Eleanor, execs. of Thomas Todd (43:375)
299. Maddy, John, m. by 5 May 1712, Ann, execs. of Robert Gardner (41:12, 364)
300. Mahan, Edward, m. by 1 July 1718, Ann, execs. of Samuel Greening (41:276)
301. Marsh, (---), m. by 14 Oct. 1727, Ann, daughter of Richard King (12:20)
302. Matthews, John, m. by 7 May 1741, Ann, daughter of Col. James Maxwell (44:75)
303. Maxwell, Samuel, m. by 29 Sept. 1720, (---), daughter and admnx. of Henry King (42:15)
304. McComas, Alexander, m. by 27 July 1747, Deborah, admnx. of Thomas Deaver (44:73, 174)
305. McComas, John, m. by June 1713, Ann, extx. of John Edwards (30:383)
306. McComas, John, m. by March 1719/20, Ann, mother of Julian Love (32:280)
307. McDaniel, Charles, m. by 2 July 1725, Johanna, widow and extx. of James Barlow (43:21, 68; Md. Cal. Wills, V, 74)
308. McDaniel, Hugh, of P.G. Co., m. by 13 March 1737, Elizabeth, relict of John Yates of Balto. Co. (16:61)

BALTIMORE COUNTY MARRIAGE REFERENCES 1659 - 1746

309. McKinsey, Jno., m. by 8 Nov. 1723, Eleanor, daughter of Henry Donahue (41:129, 176)
310. Mcackelday, John, m. by March 1719/20, Ann, extx. of Robert Gardner (32:342) [see #299]
311. Massey, Edward, m. by March 1717/8, Ann, admnx. of Samuel Greening (31:253)
312. Mathews, Thomas, m. by Nov. 1718, Sarah, extx. of John Thomas (31:55)
313. Mead, Edward, m. by 6 Nov. 1746, Darkes, daughter of John Ewings (20:188)
314. Medcalfe, John, dec., m. by 10 June 1740, (---), daughter of John Norris of Anne Arundel Co. (16:397)
315. Merriken, Hugh, m. by 23 Dec. 1719, Ann, extx. of George Westall (41:46, 47)
316. Merriken, Joshua, m. by 4 Nov. 1720, Dinah, daughter and legatee of Nicholas Day (9:251)
317. Merryman, (---), m. by 24 June 1702, Jane, formerly wife of Joseph Peake, and extx. of Jane Long (42:34, 216)
318. Merryman, (---), m. by 19 Nov. 1709, Mary, daughter of Humphrey Boone (Md. Cal. Wills, III, 156)
319. Miles (---), m. by 7 Jan. 1733/4, Mary, mother of John Miles Youngblood (15:16)
320. Moorcock, (---), m. by 13 July 1734, Susannah, mother of Thomas Demmett (15:85)
321. Moore, James, m. by 20 April 1732, Frances, admnx. of John Gay (42:12)
322. Morgan, John, m. by 9 Dec. 1745, Flora, widow of Joseph Peregoy (45:37)
323. Morris, Thomas, m. by June 1711, (---), widow of Simeon Jackson (30:210)
324. Mountfield, John, m. by 18 June 1698, Ann, formerly wife of Thomas Morris (3:251)
325. Murphy Edward, of Cecil Co., m. by 2 Oct 1715, Jane, daughter of Thomas Greenfield (8:376)
326. Murray, Josephus, Jr., m. by 20 Aug. 1747, Margaret, widow of John Rattenbury (44:168)
327. Newman, Dennis, m. by 19 Sept. 1709, Katherine, widow and extx. of Thomas Knightsmith (42:104)

BALTIMORE COUNTY MARRIAGE REFERENCES 1659 - 1746

328. Noland, Thomas, m. by 23 Sept. 1713, Mary, (prob.daughter and) coheir of Matthew Hawkins (10:208)
329. Norton, (---), m. by 23 Oct 1735, Elizabeth, mother of Ford Barnes (15:323)
330. Norwood, (---), m. by Nov 1728, Ruth, sister of Richard Owings (13:113)
331. Norwood, John, m. by 13 Sept. 1726, Rachel, admnx. of Benjamin Lawrence (43:57)
332. Ogg, Francis, m. by June 1710, Katherine, admnx. of Henry Rhodes (30:156)
333. Ogg, Francis, m. by 7 Sept. 1723, Mary, admins. of William Beard (42:323; 43:61; 51:23)
334. Ogle, John, m. by 24 June 1743, Rosanna, poss. widow of Jonas Robinson, and admnx. of John Bowen (43:259, 310)
335. Oldton, John, m. by Sept. 1693, Ann, extx. of David Jones (29:126)
336. Oless, Robert, m. by 4 June 1695, Margaret, daughter of Thomas O'Daniel, and widow of William Westbury (1:466)
337. Olwell(?), John, m. by 10 April 1711, Elizabeth, late wife of William Geff of Baltimore Co. (8:162)
338. Organ, Matthew, m. by 23 April 1705, Katherine, widow and admnx. of Yarlo Michael Owen (42:166, 227)
339. Osaborne, William, m. by March 1693/4, Margaret, extx. of John Walstone (29:205)
340. Osborne, William, d. by 5 Nov. 1724 having m. Avarilla, sister of William Hollis (11:28)
341. Osborne, William, m. by 7 Nov. 1734, Catherine, sister of Henry Rhodes (15:131)
342. Paca, (---), m. by 5 Oct. 1746, Elizabeth, daughter of Thomas Sheredine (20:185)
343. Paca, (---), m. by 25 May (----), Martha, daughter of James Phillips the Elder (42:266)
344. Paca, Aquila, m. by 4 Nov. 1725, Frances, daughter of John Stokes (11:200)
345. Paca, John, m. by 20 Oct. 1736, Eliza, extx. of William Smith (43:216)
346. Pacquinett, Michael, of Bath Co., N.C., m. by 12 Feb. 1727, Charity, daughter of Richard Tydings (12:61)
347. Parker, John, m. by 3 Oct 1704, Isabella, admins. of Thomas Smith (42:186)

BALTIMORE COUNTY MARRIAGE REFERENCES 1659 - 1746

348. Parker, John, of Calvert Co., m. by 12 March 1724, Mary, daughter of Christopher Beanes of Calvert Co. (11:101)
349. Parlett, (---), m. by 3 Feb. 1734, Mary, daughter of Henry Pitch (15:166)
350. Parrish, Edward, m. by 13 Aug. 1736, Elizabeth, daughter of Stephen Gill (43:220)
351. Peake, Joseph, m. by 6 March 1697, Jane, execs. of Jane Long (42:34)
352. Peters, John, m. by Oct. 1701, Hester, mother of John Fuller (7:93)
353. Phillips, Col. James, d. by 12 Dec. 1720; his widow Johanna was the mother of John and Richard Kemp (9:287)
354. Pickett, Heathcote, m. by 27 July 1743, Elizabeth, widow of William Wright, and James Greer (43:267, 312)
355. Pickett, William, m. by c.1700, (---), heiress of Joseph Heathcote (26:41)
356. Pickett, William, m. by 8 Sept 1724, (---) widow of Gideon Skates (43:15)
357. Pierpoint, Charles, m. by 4 June 1721, Sydney, sister of William Chew of Baltimore Co. (Md. Inv., 5:87)
358. Pike, William, m. by 7 Sept. 1741, Ann, admnx. of Abraham Whitaker (44:120)
359. Pissons, of Pitstow, William, or Philip, m. by Nov. 1692, Ann, relict of William Pearce (28:307)
360. Plummer, Thomas, of Prince Georges Co., m. by 26 Aug. 1703, Elizabeth, daughter of George Yate of Anne Arundel Co. (7:309)
361. Pottee, Lewis, Jr., m. by 2 Nov. 1726, Catherine, daughter and coheir of Matthew Green (11:290)
362. Powell, James, m. by 21 Jan. 1724, Rebecca, extx. of Col. Richard Colegate (11:9; 41:322)
363. Powell, James, m. by 17 Oct. 1737, Eleanor, daughter of Richard Hewitt (43:250).
364. Powell, John, m. by 15 May 1734, Elizabeth, relict of John Poteet, Sr. (15:55)
365. Power, James, of Cecil Co., m. by 24 March 1746, Sarah, daughter of George Linager (20:537)
366. Presbury, George, m. by 5 March 1745, Isabella, daughter of Wm. Robinson (20:34)
367. Presbury, George, m. by Aug. 1746 the extx. of John Bond who left a daughter Elizabeth (Balttimore Co. Court Proc., TB#TR #1, p.210)
368. Preston, James, m. by 9 July 1725, Sarah, daughter of Daniel Scott (43:18)

BALTIMORE COUNTY MARRIAGE REFERENCES 1659 - 1746

369. Price, Benjamin, m. by 17 Oct 1737, Elizabeth, widow of Richard Hewitt (43:250)
370. Prichard, Herbert, m. by 23 Jan 172?, Mary, daughter of John Order (10:81)
371. Pumphrey, (---), m. by 23 Feb. 1724, Mary, widow of William Cockey (11:32)
372. Puntenay, (---), m. by 8 Jan. 1730, Ann, daughter of Edward Parrish (14:50)
373. Ramsey, Charles, m. by 1 March 1691, Elizabeth, widow of John Walley and daughter of Thomas Thurston (1:340, 356; 28:152)
374. Ramsey, John, m. by 1 Dec. 1744, Johanna, admins. of William Potee (45:4)
375. Randall, Christopher, m. by 14 Jan. 1722, Ann, sister of William Chew of Baltimore Co. (45:4)
376. Raven, Luke, m. by 21 April 1728, Sarah, daughter of Thomas(?) Major(?) (42:309)
377. Raven, Luke, m. by 13 March 1724/5, Elizabeth, daughter of Thomas and Mary Hughes (11:30)
378. Reeves, Edward, m. by Aug. 1683, Henrietta, widow of Thomas Cannon and William Robinson (1; 27:187)
379. Reynolds, John, m. by 30 May 1695, Providence, widow of (---) Davidge (1:470)
380. Rhoades, William, m. by 24 Nov 1731, Mary, daughter of Henry Matthews (14:185)
381. Richardson, Daniel, m. by 13 Sept. 1709, Elizabeth, daughter of John Welch or Welsh (8:33)
382. Richardson, Mark, m. by June 1683, (---) widow of George Utie (27:45)
383. Richardson, Thomas, m. by 9 May 1685, Rachel, admnx. of John Tower (1:216)
384. Rigbie, Nathan, m. by 26 July 1734, Cassandra, daughter of Philip Coale (43:172)
385. Rigdon, John, m. by 23 Aug. 1742, (---), daughter of William Bond (43:271)
386. Risteau, John, m. by 16 Dec. 1723, Catherine, widow and relict of William Talbott, and daughter of George Ogg, Sr. (3:377; 10:232)
387. Roberts, John, m. by 13 Feb. 1705, Mary, widow of Thomas Jackson (6:20)

BALTIMORE COUNTY MARRIAGE REFERENCES 1659 - 1746

388. Robertson, Robert, m. by 2 July 1723, Sarah, widow of Martin Taylor (41:110)
389. Robinson, John, m. by 8 May 1744, Mary, admins. of Philip Jarvis (43:380)
390. Rogers, William, m. by 13 Aug. 1736, (---), daughter of Stephen Gill (43:220)
391. Rowles, Jacob, m. by 14 Jan. 1722, Patience, widow of Nathaniel Stinchcomb.
392. Royston, John, m. by 10 March 1697, Anne, widow and extx. of Roland Thornborough (Inv. and Accts., 16:25)
393. Ruff, Richard, m. c1700, (---), heiress of Daniel Peverell (26:20)
394. Russell, Francis, m. by 1 Aug. 1732, Elizabeth, mother of John Ryley (14:267)
395. Sater, Henry, m. by June 1718, Mary, admnx. of Edward Stevenson (31:316)
396. Saunders, Robert, of ANNE ARUNDEL Co., m. by 4 June 1745, Rebecca, sister of Moses Groome (19:338)
397. Savage, Hill, m. by March 1718/9, Eleanor, extx. of Peter Bond (31:74)
398. Scott, Daniel, m. by 14 March 1709, Eliza, extx. of Robert Love (42:109)
399. Scott, Daniel, m. by 31 March 1744, Jane Johnson, sister of Elizabeth Shaw, and daughter of Deborah Benger (18:471)
400. Scott, Daniel, Jr., m. by 15 March 1742, Hannah, daughter of Isaac Butterworth (17:196)
401. Scott, Nathaniel, m. by 31 March 1741, Abarilla, daughter of Luke Raven 18:471)
402. Scrivener, William, m. by 30 March 1744, Elizabeth, coheir of John Clarke who was a son of Matthew Clarke (18:565)
403. Seabrooke, William, m. by 26 March 1742, Jemima, sister of Christopher Gist (17:132)
404. Sergeant, John, m. by 4 Aug. 1737, Elizabeth; admins. of Thomas Gostwick (43:229)
405. Shavers, Abraham, m. by Aug. 1718, Mary, extx. of Henry Dukes (31:19)
406. Simmons, Charles, m. (---), admnx of Thomas Jones (42:238)
407. Sindall, Philip, m. by 22 July 1721, Catherine, daughter of Jacob and Jane Peacock (41:203, 239)

BALTIMORE COUNTY MARRIAGE REFERENCES 1659 - 1746

408. Skipwith, George, m. by 27 Oct. 1676, Eliz., daughter of Thomas Thurston (1:55, 60; 4:331)
409. Smith, Edward, m. by 23 Oct. 1711, Margaret, admnx. of Charles Jones (41:297)
410. Smith, John, m. by 22 Feb. 1719, Dorothy, widow and admnx. of Thomas Williamson (32:626; 41:52, 331)
411. Smith, William, m. by 29 Oct. 1730, Elizabeth, admins. of Richard Dallam (42:253)
412. Smith, Winston, m. by 19 Dec. 1743, Susanna, extx. of George Stokes (43:331)
413. Smithers, Richard, m. by 25 May ????, Mary, daughter of James Phillips, the Elder (42:266)
414. Smithson, Owen, m. by 2 May 1732, Ann, daughter of Thomas Jackson, and mother of James Bisco (14:256)
415. Smithson, Thomas, m. by 9 July 1725, Ann, daughter of Daniel Scott (43:18)
416. Staley, (---), m. by 25 April 1701, Mary, widow of Thomas Jones (7:105)
417. Stamford, James, m. by 15 Nov. 1727, Mary, mother of John Fuller (12:28)
418. Stand, or Hand, John, m. by 14 Feb. 1732, Rosanna, daughter of Jacob Grove (43:108)
419. Stand, John, m. by 2 June 1736, Elizabeth, sister of John Durham (15:361)
420. Standiford, William, m. by 16 April 1742, Christiana, admins. of Thomas Wright (43:308)
421. Stansbury, Dixon, m. by 9 May 1744, Penelope, daughter of Stephen Body (43:372)
422. Stewart, James, m. by 27 May 1742, Mary, admnx. of Joshua Wood (45:168)
423. Stinchcomb, John, m. by 26 Jan 1738, Katherine, daughter of Hector McLane (16:122)
424. Stockett, Thomas, m. by 17 March 1708, Damaris, daughter of John Welch (8:5)
425. Stokes, George, m. by 14 Sept. 1741, Susannah, daughter of Col. James Phillips (17:42)
426. Stokes, John, m. by 7 Nov. 1723, Susanna, daughter of George Wells (10:212; 14:418)

BALTIMORE COUNTY MARRIAGE REFERENCES 1659 - 1746

427. Stone, (---), of Chas. Co., dec., m. by 4 Feb. 1739, Mary, daughter of Richard Boughton (16:341)
428. Stone, Thomas, m. by Aug. 1720, Elizabeth, widow of Samuel Hinton and extx. of Richard Sampson (32:259; 41:225)
429. Stone, Thomas, m. by 26 May 1735, Elizabeth, formerly wife of James Bagford (15:237)
430. Strawbridge, Joseph, m. by 17 Sept. 1696, Sarah, extx. of John Arden (Inv. and Accts., 14:152)
431. Swann, Thomas, of St. Mary's Co., m. by 17 Nov. 1745, Elizabeth, daughter of Edward Boteler (19:389)
432. Swinyard, John, m. by 8 Oct. 1712, Luch, execs. of Francis Potee (41:354)
433. Talbie, Samuel, m. by 5 Dec. 1744, Elizabeth, daughter of William Hitchcock (18:664)
434. Talbot, John, m. by 10 Jan. 1726/7, (---) daughter of Col. Richard Colegate (41:322)
435. Talbot, William, d. by 16 Dec. 1723, leaving widow Catherine (daughter of George Ogg) who m. 2nd John Risteau (3:377; 10:232)
436. Talbot, William, m. by 19 June 1731, Mary, daughter of John Roberts (43:99)
437. Taylor, Arthur, m. by 6 Mach 1683, Frances, mother of James Smithers (1:68)
438. Taylor, Francis, c1729, antenuptial contract with Elizabeth Whiteacre (13:109)
439. Taylor, James, m. by 15 July 1739, Mary, widow of John Thomas (16:230)
440. Taylor, James, m. 1st Mary Foster, now dec.; on 4 May 1747 about to marry Sarah, daughter of Rowland Kemble (20:380)
441. Taylor, John, m. by June 1711, Elizabeth, extx. of William Peckett (30:213, 216)
442. Taylor, John, m. by 9 March 1732/3, Mary, relict of Edward Talbott (14:392)
443. Taylor, Thomas, m. by June 1714, Elizabeth, extx. of Edward Welsh (30:513)
444. Taylor, Thomas, m. by 20 Feb. 1729, (---), daughter of Mary Price (42:247)
445. Tayman, Benjamin, m. by 2 Aug. 1736, Sarah Cockey, widow of Joshua Cockey, grandmother of Sarah Hanson (19:311; 43:221)

BALTIMORE COUNTY MARRIAGE REFERENCES 1659 - 1746

446. Teall, Edward, m. by 28 Feb. 1721, Hannah, widow of Nathaniel Stinchcomb (9:209; 30:274, 297)
447. Thomas, (---), m. by 13 June 1720, Jane, sister of Richard Freeborne (1:661)
448. Thomas, David, m. by 1716, Hannah, poss. widow of George Smith (8:477)
449. Thomas, David, m. by 27 June 1721, Ann, sister of Richard Freeborne (41:244, 260)
450. Thomas, David, m. by 15 Sept. 1741, Elizabeth, daughter of Benjamin Wheeler (16:555)
451. Thorpe, Edward, m. by 1 July 1737, Catherine, widow and extx. of Thomas Cullins (43:234; Md. Cal. Wills, VI, 216)
452. Thurcall, Thomas, m. by 27 July 1686, Jane, daughter of Thomas O'Daniel (1:188; 27:164)
453. Tipper, Edgar, m. by March 1714/5, Elizabeth, admnx. of William Pritchard (30:612)
454. Todd, (---), m. by 18 Jan. 1676/7, Anna, sister of Charles Gorsuch (3:57)
455. Todd, Launcelot, of ANNE ARUNDEL Co., m. by 5 March 1683, Sarah, daughter and heiress of Thomas Phelps of Anne Arundel Co., deceased (1:116)
456. Tolley, (---), m. by 13 June 1720, Mary, sister of Richard Freeborne (1:661)
457. Toogood, Josias, of ANNE ARUNDEL Co., m. by 13 Sept. 1709, Mary, daughter of John Welsh (8:33)
458. Touchstone, Richard, m. by 23 Oct. 1736, (---), daughter of Daniel Johnson (43:224)
459. Townsend, John, m. by 26 May 1733, Amy, admnx. of Hector McLane (43:126)
460. Treadway, Richard, m. by June 1713, Jane, mother of John Smith (30:379)
461. Tye, John, m. by 12 Feb. 1736, Persesha, daughter of George Hitchcock (3:356)
462. Utie, George, m. by 30 Dec. 1696, Mary, daughter of Edward Bedell (3:80, 241)
463. Van Deaver, Jacob, m. by 26 Nov 1718, Jane, widow of John Gill (42:142)

BALTIMORE COUNTY MARRIAGE REFERENCES 1659 - 1746

464. Walker, (---), m. by 12 Oct. 1745, Mary, mother of Mary Hanson (19:363)
465. Walley, John, d. by March 1691/2; m. Elizabeth, daughter of Thomas Thurston; she m. 2nd Charles Ramsey (28:152)
466. Wallford, John, m. by Nov. 1693, Mary, extx. of John Nicholson (29:165)
467. Wallox, John, m. by 4 Sept. 1742, Eliza, widow of Jacob Jones (43:291)
468. Warfoote, (---), m. by 2 Sept. 1696, Mary, extx. of John Nicholson or William Nicholson (42:33; Inv. and Accts., 14:154, 155)
469. Warren, Thomas, d. by 27 May 1736, having m. Mary, mother of Thomas, Lewis, and Jonathan Jones (16:69-71)
470. Washington, Philip, m. by 14 May 1707, Alice, extx. of Peter Bond (42:82)
471. Watkins, Francis, m. by 7 June 1681, Christiana Wright, whose mother m. Thomas Long (6:121)
472. Watkins, John, m. by 9 Nov. 1742, Margaret, daughter of William Loney (43:263)
473. Webster, (---), m. by 3 March 1728, Elizabeth, daughter of Nathaniel Giles (12:283)
474. Wells, Charles, m. by 3 June 1726, Sarah, admnx. of John Wright (43:60)
475. Wells, George, m. by 6 July 1708, Mary, extx. of Robert Gibson (42:121)
476. Wesley, John, m. by 8 June 1722, Mary, widow and admnx. of John Bond (41:229; Baltimore Co. Wills, 1:169)
477. West, John, of Prince Georges Co., joiner, m. by 22 March 1730, Ann Dewes? (14:88)
478. West, John, m. by 3 Nov. 1743, Ann Dew (18:358)
479. Westbury, William, d. by 4 June 1695, having m. Margaret, prob. daughter of Thomas O'Daniel; she m. 2nd Robert Oless (1:466)
480. Whayland, Patrick, m. by 2 Nov 1726, Catherine, daughter of Henry Matthews (14:208; 50:66)
481. Wheeler, Solomon, copy of Quaker marr. cert. dated 22 day, 11, 1745, to Rachel Taylor (Chattel Record TR#E, p.210)
482. Wheeler, William, Jr., m. by 20 Feb 1729, Constant, admnx. of Stephen Price (42:247)
483. White, Thomas, m. by 3 June 1731, Sophia, daughter of John Hall (14:105)

BALTIMORE COUNTY MARRIAGE REFERENCES 1659 - 1746

484. Wilkinson, William, m. by Sept. 1684, Elizabeth, heir of Abraham and Sarah Clark (1:199; 27:199)
485. Williams, Lodowick, m. by 9 March 1673, Mary, daughter of James Stringer and w. Ann who m. 2nd John Collier, and 3rd William York (Test.Proc., 6:42)
486. Windley, Richard, m. by 5 June 1695, Mary, sister of Arthur Taylor (1:461; 29:220)
487. Wise, William, m. by 8 March 1705, Margaret, extx. of William Osborne (42:243)
488. Wolley, John, d. by 1 March 1691, his widow Elizabeth (daughter of Thomas Thurston), m. 2nd Charles Ramsey (1:340, 356)
489. Wood, John, m. by 5 Sept. 1688, Elizabeth, daughter of Edward Swanson (6:67)
490. Woodfield, Thomas, m. by 13 March 1717, Elizabeth, daughter of Anthony Holland; she may have m. 1st (---) Gott (8:544)
491. Worrell, (---), m. by 6 June 1745, Mary, mother of Erick White (19:112)
492. Worthington, (---), m. by 20 June 1743, Hannah, mother of Margaret, John, Hannah, and Anne Cromwell (43:318)
493. Wright, John, antenuptial contract dated 16 May 1685, with widow Jane Claridge (1:136)
494. Yeats, Humphrey, m.by 2 Sept. 1725, Lawrana, admins. of Henry Shields (43:37)
495. Yeo, (---), m. by 20 Sept. 1686, Somelia, relict and admnx. of Ruthen Garrettson (42:37)
496. York, George, m. by 5 March 1744, Elinor, daughter of James Hackett (19:49)
497. York, William, m. by 9 March 1673, Ann, widow of James Stringer and John Collier, and mother of Mary who m. Lodowick Williams (Testamentary Proceedings, 6:42)
498. York, William, m. by June 1692, the relict of John Wood (28:186, 187)
499. York, William, m. by Sept 1695, the extx. of Jacob Lotton (29:490)
500. Young, William, m. by 1 Aug. 1737, Clare Tasker (3:481)

INDEX

-A-
ADDAMS,
  Richard*, 88
  Susannah, 88
  William, 88
ANDERSON,
  Jane, 61
  John*, 61
ARDEN,
  John*, 430
  Sarah, 430
ARMSTRONG,
  James, 31
  Widow, 31
ARNOLD,
  Mary ?, 75
  Susanna, 75
AYRES,
  Edmund, 114
  Elizabeth, 114

-B-
BAGFORD,
  Elizabeth, 429
  James, 429
BALL,
  Hannah, 135
  Richard, 135
BANKSON,
  Hannah, 243
  Joseph*, 243
BARLOW,
  Bathsheba, 199
  James, 199
  James*, 307
  Johanna, 307
BARNES,
  Elizabeth, 329
  Ford, 329
BARTON,
  Abagail, 228
  daughter, 228
BAYS, Ruth, 50
BEANES,
  Ann, 95

Christopher, 95, 348
Mary, 348
BEARD,
  Mary, 333
  William*, 333
BEDELL,
  Edward, 184, 462
  Martha, 184
  Mary, 462
BENGER, Deborah, 399
BENNETT,
  Benjamin, 22
  Elizabeth, 34
  Richard, 34
  Sarah, 22
BENSON,
  Daniel, 159, 237
  Elizabeth, 159
  Jane, 237
BISCO,
  Ann, 414
  James, 414
BISHOP,
  Elizabeth, 109
  Robert, 109
BODY,
  Penelope, 421
  Stephen, 421
BOND,
  Alice, 470
  Clemency, 37
  daug of, 262
  Daughter, 3
  daughter, 385
  Eleanor, 397
  Elizabeth, 367
  Else, 261
  Hester, 238
  John, 367, 476
  Mary, 476
  Peter*, 238, 397, 470
  Sarah, 291, 293
  William, 3, 261, 262,
    291, 293, 385
BOONE,

Hunphrey, 318
Jane, 174
Mary, 174, 318
BOOTHBY,
  Edward, 258
  Elizabeth, 258
BOREING,
  James*, 148
  Rebecca, 148
BOTELER,
  Edward, 431
  Elizabeth, 431
BOUGHTON,
  Mary, 427
  Richard, 427
BOWEN,
  John*, 334
  Jonas, 171, 297
  Martha, 297
  Rebecca, 171
  Rosanna, 334
BRADSHAW,
  John, 104
  Mary, 104
BROAD,
  Jane, 96
  John, 96
BROOKE, Mary, 248
BROWN,
  Eliz., 66
  John, 66
BUTLER,
  Edward*, 211
  Martha, 211
BUTTERWORTH,
  dau of, 39
  Hannah, 400
  Isaac, 39, 155, 400
  Mary, 155

-C-
CANNON,
  Henrietta, 378
  Thomas, 378
CANTWELL,

27

Edward*, 63
Joan, 63
CHADWELL,
  John, Sr.*, 265
  Margaret, 265
CHEW,
  Ann, 375
  Margaret, 57
  Sydney, 357
  William, 57, 357, 375
CHOICE,
  Jane, 128
  William, 128
CLARIDGE, Jane, 493
CLARK,
  Abraham, 225
  Abraham*, 484
  Elizabeth, 484
  John, 72
  John*, 181
  Lewsey, 72
  Mary, 181, 225
  Mathew, 72
  Sarah, 225
  Sarah*, 484
CLARKE,
  Eliz., 402
  John*, 402
  Matthew, 402
CLARKSON,
  Milcah, 48
  Robert, 48
COALE,
  Cassandra, 384
  Philip, 384
COCKEY,
  Joshua, 445
  Mary, 371
  Sarah, 156, 445
  William, 371
COLE,
  Barbara, 53
  Sarah, 170
  Thomas*, 170
COLEGATE,
  Col.Richard, 62, 434
  Col.Richard*, 362

Patience, 62
Rebecca, 362
COLLIER,
  Ann, 183, 497
  John, 183, 485, 497
  Sarah, 183
CONSTANT,
  John, Sr., 52
  Sarah, 52
COX,
  Christopher, 33, 109
  Elizabeth, 33, 45, 109
  Mary, 33, 109
  William, 45
CRABTREE,
  Grace, 208
  Mary, 210
  William, 208, 210
CRANDON, Dorothy, 36
CRASHOW,
  Elizabeth, 202
  William, 202
CROMWELL,
  Anne, 492
  Elizabeth, 7
  Hannah, 492
  John, 492
  Margaret, 492
  Thomas, 7
  William, 7
CROOK,
  Chloe, 105
  James, 105
CULLINS,
  Catherine, 451
  Thomas, 451
CURRIER, Thomas*, 248

-D-
DALLAM,
  Eliabeth, 411
  Richard*, 411
DANIEL,
  Charles*, 227
  Rachel, 227
DAVIDGE, Providence, 379
DAY,
  Dinah, 316
  Elizabeth, 33
  Nicholas, 33, 316
DEATH,
  Randall, 111
  Rebecca, 111
DEAVER,
  Deborah, 304
  Thomas*, 304
DELAP,
  Abraham*, 253
  Widow of, 253
DEMMETT,
  Susannah, 320
  Thomas, 320
DEMONDIDIER,
  Anthony, 172
  Elizabeth, 172
DEW, Ann, 478
DEWES, Ann, 477
DISON,
  Elizabeth, 113
  William, 113
DITTO,
  Abraham, 153
  Christiana, 153
DONAHUE,
  Eleanor, 309
  Henry, 309
DORSEY,
  Capt.John, 175
  Col.Edward, 252
  Edward*, 175
  Margaret, 252
  Ruth, 175
DOWER,
  Edward*, 255
  Mary, 255
DOWSE,
  Edward*, 255, 267
  Mary, 255
DOYNE,
  Robert, 250
  Sarah, 250
DREW,

Anthony, 280, 286
Bethia, 286
Susannah, 280
DUKES,
  Henry*, 405
  Mary, 405
DULEY,
  Blanch, 23
  William, 23
DURBIN,
  Christopher*, 122
  Mary, 122
DURHAM,
  Elizabeth, 419
  John, 41, 419
  Widow, 41
DUSKINS,
  Dennis, 147
  Mary, 147

-E-
EBDEN,
  Jane, 268
  William, 268
EDWARDS,
  Ann, 305
  John*, 305
EMISON,
  James*, 80
  Rebecca, 80
ENGLISH,
  Ann, 58
  Dennis*, 58
ENLOES,
  Abraham, 127
  Abraham*, 131
  Elizabeth, 131, 281
  John*, 281
  Margaret, 127
EWINGS,
  Darkes, 313
  John, 313

-F-
FARFARR,
  Christiana, 269
  William, 269

FITCH,
  Henry, 349
  Mary, 349
FITZREDMOND,
  Barbara, 69
  John, 69
FORD,
  Elizabeth, 79
  James, 79
  John, 11
  Mary, 11
FOSTER, Mary, 440
FOXON,
  relict, 76
  Richard, 76
FREEBORN(E),
  Ann, 449
  Elizabeth, 157
  Jane, 447
  Mary, 456
  Priscilla, 235
  Richard, 157, 447, 449, 456
  Richard*, 235
FUGATE, Mary, 274
FULLER,
  Hester, 352
  John, 352, 417
  Mary, 417

-G-
GALLOWAY,
  Margaret, 127
  William, 127
GARDNER,
  Ann, 299, 310
  Robert*, 299, 310
GARRETT,
  Barbara, 54
  Dennis, 54
GARRETTSON,
  Ruthen, 495
  Somelia, 495
GAY,
  Frances, 321
  John*, 321
GEFF,

Elizabeth, 337
William, 337
GIBSON,
  Mary, 475
  Robert*, 475
GILBERT,
  Garvis, 259
  Mary, 259
GILES,
  Elizabeth, 473
  Nathaniel, 473
GILL,
  daughter, 390
  Elizabeth, 350
  Jane, 463
  John, 463
  Stephen, 350, 390
GILLETT,
  Ambrose, 149, 234
  Jane, 149, 234
GIST,
  Christopher, 403
  Christopher*, 40
  Edith, 40
  Jemima, 403
GITTINGS,
  Margaret, 296
  Mary, 296
GOLDSMITH, George*, 184
GORSUCH,
  Anna, 454
  Charles, 454
GOSTWICK,
  Abagail, 101
  Abarilla, 101
  Elizabeth, 404
  Nicholas, 101
  Thomas*, 404
GRANT,
  Frances, 146
  Hugh*, 146
GREEN,
  Catherine, 361
  Martha, 219
  Matthew, 219, 361
GREENFIELD,

Jane, 325
Mary, 110
Thomas, 110, 325
GREENING,
  Ann, 300, 311
  Samuel*, 300, 311
GREER,
  Elizabeth, 354
  James, 354
GROOME,
  Ann, 140, 260
  Elizabeth, 136
  Moses, 136, 140, 260, 396
  Rebecca, 396
GROOMS,
  Dorothy, 102
  Moses*, 102
GROVE,
  Jacob, 192, 418
  Rosanna, 192, 418
GWINS,
  Mary, 187
  Thomas, 187

-H-
HACKETT,
  Elinor, 496
  James, 496
HAILE,
  Nicholas, 173
  Susannah, 173
HALE,
  Diana, 21
  Mathew*, 21
HALL,
  Diana, 21
  Frances, 116
  Francis, 116
  John, 67, 87, 116, 483
  Matthew*, 21
  Sarah, 67, 87
  Sophia, 483
HAND, Rosanna, 192
HANSON,
  Mary, 464

Sarah, 156, 445
HARRIS,
  Elinor, 118
  Elizabeth, 99
  William, 99, 118
HARRISON, Mary, 267
HARRYMAN,
  Eleanor, 138
  John*, 138
HASTINGS, John*, 133
HAWKINS,
  Ann, 130
  Anna, 56
  Diana, 82
  Mary, 328
  Mathew, 56, 328
  Matthew*, 82
  William, 130
HEATHCOTE,
  John, 119
  Joseph*, 141, 355
  Martha, 141
  Sylvia, 119
HERBERT,
  Eleanor, 84
  Rebecca, 84
HEWITT,
  Eleanor, 363
  Elizabeth, 369
  Richard, 363, 369
HICKS, Jane, 103
HIGGINSON,
  Ann, 35
  John*, 35
HILL,
  Mary, 282
  Rachael, 144
  William, 144
  William*, 282
HINTON,
  Elizabeth, 428
  Samuel, 428
HITCHCOCK,
  Ann, 19, 73
  Elizabeth, 433
  George, 461
  Persesha, 461

Philisana, 218
  William, 19, 73, 218, 433
HOLLAND,
  Anthony, 490
  Elizabeth, 490
HOLLIDAY,
  James*, 277
  Sarah, 277
HOLLIS,
  Avarilla, 340
  daughter, 77
  relect, 201
  William, 77, 340
  William*, 201
HOLMAN,
  Abraham*, 182
  Sarah, 182
HOOPER,
  George, 87
  George*, 183
  Isabella, 183
  Sarah, 87
HOPE,
  George*, 207, 230
  Judith, 207, 230
HORNER,
  Ann, 24
  Nicholas*, 24
HOWARD,
  Anne, 232
  Charles, 224
  Edward, 232
  Joshua*, 168, 169
  Martha, 65
  Mary, 168, 224
  Violetta, 169
  William, 65
HOWE,
  Rebecca, 162
  Sarah, 162
HUGHES,
  Elizabeth, 377
  Margaret, 193
  Mary, 193, 377
  Samuel, 193
  Thomas, 377

HUMPHREYS,
  Mary, 14
  Thomas, 14
HUTCHINGS,
  Diana, 21
  William*, 21

-I-
ISRAEL,
  John, 212
  Sarah, 212

-J-
JACKSON,
  Ann, 32, 414
  Mary, 387
  Simeon, 323
  Thomas, 32, 387, 414
  widow, 323
JAMES,
  Margaret, 220
  Mary, 220
  Thomas*, 220
JARVIS,
  Mary*, 389
  Philip, 389
JOHNS,
  Abraham*, 185
  Hannah, 185
JOHNSON,
  Andrew, 74
  Ann, 140
  Anthony, 233
  Capt.Henry, 42
  Catherine, 233
  Daniel, 70, 71, 97, 134, 458
  Daniel*, 145
  Daughter, 71, 97, 134
  daughter, 70, 458
  Elizabeth, 42, 74
  Frances, 145
  Jane, 27, 399
  Rachel, 133
  Stephen, 140
JONES,
  Ann, 335

Charles*, 409
David*, 335
Edward*, 205
Elinor, 279
Eliza, 467
Elizabeth, 245, 246
Henry, 246
Henry*, 245
Jacob, 467
Jonathan, 469
Lewis, 469
Margaret, 409
Mary, 288, 416, 469
Rachel, 215
Rathvael, 215
Sarah, 205
Solomon, 279
Thomas, 215, 416, 469
Thomas*, 288, 406

-K-
KEMB, Elizabeth, 51
KEMBLE,
  Rowland, 440
  Sarah, 440
KEMP,
  Johanna, 353
  John, 353
  Richard, 353
KEYS, Francis*, 285
KING,
  Ann, 301
  daughter, 303
  Henry*, 303
  Richard, 301
KINSEY,
  Elizabeth, 257
  Paul, 257
KNIGHTSMITH,
  Katherine, 327
  Thomas, 327

-L-
LAWRENCE,
  Benjamin*, 331
  Rachel, 331
LEA,

Alice, 287
John*, 287
LEAKINS,
  John*, 236
  Margaret, 236
LEE,
  John, 126
  Mary, 126
LIGHTFOOT,
  Rebecca, 191
  Thomas, 191
LINAGER,
  George, 365
  Sarah, 365
LITTLE,
  Elizabeth, 139
  James, 139
LOGSDON,
  Ann, 125
  William, 125
LONEY,
  Arabella, 154
  Daughter, 17
  Margaret, 472
  William, 17, 472
  William*, 154
LONG,
  Gavilla, 272
  Jane, 272, 351
  Jane*, 317
  Thomas, 471
LOTTON, Jacob*, 499
LOVE,
  Ann, 306
  Eliza, 398
  Julian, 306
  Robert, 30
  Robert*, 398
  Sarah, 30, 276
  William*, 276
LOWE,
  Sarah, 276
  William*, 276
LYNCH,
  Ann, 217
  Mary, 283
  Patrick, 217

Robuck, 283

-M-
MCINTOSH,
  Daniel, 203
  Margaret, 203
MCLANE,
  Amy, 459
  Hector, 423
  Hector*, 459
  Katherine, 423
MAJOR,
  Sarah, 376
  Thomas, 376
MARRYMAN, Jane, 273
MATTHEWS,
  Catherine, 480
  Henry, 380, 480
  Mary, 380
MAXWELL,
  Ann, 302
  Asael, 186
  Col.James, 302
  Hannah, 186
MENCHAM, Mary, 209
MERRYMAN, Charles, Jr.*, 273
MOALE,
  John*, 12
  Rachel, 12
MORRIS,
  Ann, 324
  Thomas, 324
MORTIMORE,
  Elizabeth, 93
  John, 93
MOULD,
  Ann, 123
  Frances, 152
  John, 123, 152
MURRAY,
  James, 98
  Jemima, 98
  Josephus, 167
  Zipporah, 167

-N-
NEWPORT,
  George*, 226
  Jane, 226
NICHOLSON,
  John*, 466, 468
  Mary, 466, 468
  William, 468
NORRIS,
  Benjamin, 240
  daughter, 314
  Elizabeth, 240
  John, 314

NORTON,
  Eliz., 204
  John*, 204
NORWOOD,
  Andrew, 20
  Elizabeth, 20
NUSOME, Helen, 13

-O-
O'DANIEL,
  Jane, 452
  Margaret, 336, 479
  Mary, 229
  Rebecca, 112
  Thomas, 112, 229, 336, 452, 479
OGG,
  Catherine, 386, 435
  George, 386, 435
OLESS,
  Margaret, 479
  Robert, 479
ORDER,
  John, 370
  Mary, 370
ORRICK,
  Hannah, 231
  William*, 231
OSBORNE,
  Margaret, 487
  William*, 487
O'TRACEY,
  Mary, 222

Tego*, 222
OVERTON,
  Jane, 180, 290
  Thomas*, 180, 290
OWEN,
  Katherine, 338
  Yarlo Michael, 338
OWINGS,
  Richard, 330
  Ruth, 330

-P-
PARISH,
  Ann, 372
  Edward, 372
PEACOCK,
  Catherine, 407
  Jacob, 407
  Jane, 407
PEAKE,
  Jane, 317
  Jemima, 55
  Joseph, 55, 68, 270, 317
  Mary, 68, 270
PEARCE, Ann, 359
PEARCH, William, 359
PEARLE,
  Ann, 29
  William, 29
PECKETT,
  Elizabeth, 441
  William*, 441
PEMBERTON,
  John*, 179
  Margaret, 179
PEREGOY,
  Flora, 322
  Joseph, 322
PERKINS,
  Mary, 25
  Richard, 25
PEVEREAL, Daniel*, 393
PHELPS,
  Sarah, 455
  Thomas*, 455

PHILLIPS,
  Col. James, 164, 425
  James, 5, 343, 413
  Johannah, 164, 353
  Mariha, 343
  Mary, 413
  Susannah, 425
  Widow, 5
PICKETT,
  Elizabeth, 176, 263
  Heathcote, 176
  Temperance, 295
  William, 263, 295
PIERPOINT,
  Ellinor, 200
  Jabez*, 200
PIFFONS,
  Ann, 29
  Phillip, 29
PINDER,
  Mary, 165, 166
  Timothy, 165, 166
POTEE,
  Francis*, 432
  Johanna, 374
  Lucy, 432
  William*, 374
POTEET,
  Elizabeth, 364
  John, 137
  John, Sr., 364
  Rebecca, 137
POWELL,
  Edward, 197
  Elizabeth, 254
  Sarah, 197
PREBLE,
  Mary, 59
  Thomas, 59
PRICE,
  Constant, 482
  daughter, 444
  Mary, 194, 444
  Mordecai, 194
  Stephen*, 482
PRITCHARD,
  Elizabeth, 453

  Joseph, 92, 142
  Mary, 92, 142
  William*, 453

-R-
RAMSEY,
  Charles, 465, 488
  Elizabeth, 465, 488
RANDALL,
  Ann, 64
  Christopher*, 64
RATTENBURY,
  John, 326
  Margaret, 326
RAVEN,
  Abarilla, 401
  Elizabeth, 221
  Luke, 177, 221, 401
  Mary, 177
REEVES,
  Edward*, 9
  Mary, 9
RHODES,
  Catherine, 341
  Henry, 341
  Henry*, 332
  Katherine, 332
RICHARDSON,
  Ann, 198
  James, 284
  Lawrence*, 198
  Mary, 284
  Susanna, 249
  Thomas*, 249
RISTEAU,
  Catherine, 435
  John, 435
ROBERTS,
  daughter, 60
  Elizabeth, 206
  John, 60, 244, 436
  John*, 239
  Lucina, 244
  Mary, 239, 244, 436
  Thomas Francis, 206
ROBERTSON,
  James, 49

  Robert, 37
  Rosanna, 49
  Sarah, 37
ROBINSON,
  Hannah, 214
  Henrietta, 378
  Isabella, 366
  Jonas, 334
  Mary, 46, 251
  Rosanna, 334
  William, 46, 214, 366, 378
  William*, 251
ROGERS,
  Ellinor, 200
  Nicholas*, 200
ROYSTON,
  John, 100
  Mary, 100
RUSSELL,
  Elizabeth, 99, 202
  Jane, 178
RUXTON,
  Frances, 158
  Mary, 47, 209
  Nathaniel, 47, 209
  Nathaniel*, 158
RYLEY,
  Elizabeth, 394
  John, 394

-S-
SAMPSON,
  Elizabeth, 428
  Richard*, 428
SCOTT,
  Ann, 415
  Avarilla, 124
  Daniel, 27, 124, 242, 368, 415
  Jane, 27, 242
  Sarah, 368
SCUTT,
  Catherine, 275
  John, 275
SHADWELL,
  John*, 28

Katherine, 28
SHAR, Christopher*, 50
SHAW, Elizabeth, 27, 399
SHEREDINE,
  Elizabeth, 342
  Sarah, 188
  Thomas, 188, 342
SHIELDS,
  Eliza, 294
  Henry, 494
  John*, 294
  Lawrana, 494
SHIPLEY,
  Adam, 16
  Keturah, 16
SIDWELL,
  Jane, 117
  Roger*, 117
SIMKINS,
  Avarilla, 190
  John, 190
SKATES,
  Catherine, 106
  Gideon, 106, 356
  Widow, 356
SMITH,
  Ann, 107
  Benjamin*, 78
  Eleanor, 2
  Eliza, 345
  George, 448
  Hannah, 448
  Isabella, 347
  Jane, 460
  John, 460
  Mary, 132
  Richard, 2, 107
  Robert, 132
  Sarah, 78
  Thomas*, 347
  William*, 345
SMITHERS,
  Frances, 437
  James, 437
SMITHSON,
  Ann, 32

Owen, 32
SPINKE, Enoch, 213
SPRYE,
  Mary, 196
  Oliver, 196
STAND, Rosanna, 192
STANDEVER,
  Mary, 38
  Samuel*, 38
STANDIFORD,
  Mary, 38
  Samuel*, 38
STANSBY,
  John, 1
  Mary, 1
STEVENS,
  Giles, 256
  Mary, 256
STEVENSON,
  Daughter, 18
  Edward*, 395
  Mary, 18, 395
STINCHCOMB,
  Hannah, 446
  Nathaniel, 391, 446
  Patience, 391
STOKES,
  Frances, 344
  George*, 412
  John, 344
  Susanna, 412
STRAWBRIDGE,
  Joseph*, 4
  Mary, 4
STRINGER,
  Ann, 86, 485, 497
  James, 86, 485, 497
  Mary, 485, 497
SWANSON,
  Edward, 489
  Elizabeth, 489
SWIFT,
  Lydia, 108
  Mark, Sr., 108

-T-
TALBOTT,

Catherine, 386
Edward, 442
Margaret, 189
Mary, 442
William, 189, 386
TASKER, Clare, 500
TAYLOR,
  Abraham, 115, 120
  Arthur, 486
  Clemency, 37
  daughter, 120
  Jane, 241
  John*, 195
  Keziah, 195
  Lettice, 115
  Martin, 37, 163, 388
  Martin, Jr., 241
  Mary, 163, 486
  Rachel, 481
  Sarah, 37, 388
TAYMAN, Sarah, 156
TEALE,
  Ales, 91
  Sarah, 91
THOMAS,
  John, 439
  John*, 312
  Mary, 439
  Sarah, 312
THORNBOROUGH,
  Anne, 392
  Roland, 392
THURSTON,
  Anne, 161
  Elizabeth, 373, 408, 465, 488
  Sarah, 292
  Thomas, 161, 292, 373, 408, 465, 488
TODD,
  Eleanor, 298
  relict, 264
  Thomas, 264
  Thomas*, 298
TOWER,
  John*, 383
  Rachel, 383

TOWSON,
  Sarah, 85
  Thomas, 85
TRIPOLIS,
  daughter, 41
  Francis, 41
TUCKER,
  Margaret, 289
  Seaborn*, 289
TYDINGS,
  Charity, 346
  Mary, 121
  Pretitia, 278
  Richard, 121, 278, 346
TYE,
  John, 26
  Susanna, 26

-U-
UTIE,
  Elizabeth, 258
  George, 223, 382
  Nathaniel, 258
  Susanna, 223
  widow, 382

-W-
WALLEY,
  Elizabeth, 373
  John, 373
WALSTON,
  Arabella, 154
  John, 154
WALSTONE,
  John*, 339
  Margaret*, 339
WATSON,
  Mary, 10
  William, 10
WEBSTER,
  John*, 247
  Mary, 247
WELCH,
  Damaris, 424
  Elizabeth, 381
  John, 381, 424

  Katherine*, 160
  Pierce, 160
WELLS,
  daughter, 150
  G., 150
  George, 426
  Susanna, 426
WELSH,
  Daniel, 43
  Edward*, 443
  Elizabeth, 381, 443
  Jane, 43
  John, 381, 457
  Mary, 457
WEST,
  Constant, 15
  Robert, 15, 89
  Sarah, 89
WESTALL,
  Ann, 315
  George*, 315
WESTBURY,
  Margaret, 336
  William, 336
WHEELER,
  Benjamin, 83, 450
  Charity, 83
  Elizabeth, 450
  Martha, 44
  William, 44
WHITAKER,
  Abraham*, 358
  Ann, 358
WHITE,
  Erick, 491
  Mary, 491
  Sarah, 94
  Stephen*, 94
WHITEACRE, Elizabeth, 438
WILKINSON, Tamar, 285
WILLIAMS,
  Hannah, 271
  Lodowich, 271, 497
  Mary, 497
WILLIAMSON,

  Dorothy, 410
  Mary, 216
  Thomas, 216, 410
WILMOT,
  Daughter, 8
  John, 8
WOOD,
  Ann, 90
  John, 498
  Joshua*, 422
  Mary, 422
  Matthew, 90
  relict, 498
WOODWARD,
  Achsah, 143
  Amos*, 143
WOOLEY,
  Hannah, 266
  John, 266
WRIGHT,
  Christiana, 420, 471
  Elizabeth, 176, 354
  John*, 474
  Sarah, 129, 474
  Thomas*, 420
  William, 176, 354
  William*, 129

-Y-
YATE,
  Elizabeth, 360
  George, 360
YATES,
  Elizabeth, 308
  John, 308
YORK,
  Mary, 151
  William, 151, 485
YOUNGBLOOD,
  John Miles, 319
  Mary, 319

www.ingramcontent.com/pod-product-compliance
Lightning Source LLC
Chambersburg PA
CBHW061518040426
42450CB00008B/1672